The Word Family Activity Book

~~~~~~~

**Fun & Easy Reproducible Activities That
Help Every Child Learn Key Word Patterns
to Become Successful Readers & Writers**

~~~~~~~

by Mary Rosenberg

SCHOLASTIC
PROFESSIONAL BOOKS

New York • Toronto • London • Auckland • Sydney
Mexico City • New Delhi • Hong Kong

Dedication

With many thanks to Tiffany Fletcher
for being a good friend and wonderful colleague.

Cover design by Norma Ortiz and Kelli Thompson
Cover artwork by Amanda Haley
Interior artwork by Rusty Fletcher
Interior design by Sydney Wright

ISBN: 0-439-19936-0
Copyright © 2001 by Mary Rosenberg

Contents

Introduction

Welcome to *The Word Family Activity Book*. This book is a valuable resource in the K-2 classroom. It's filled with activities that will help you teach your students how the most common word families "work." Research tells us that knowing word families aids children as they learn to read and write, helping them to recognize words with the same sounds and same endings. To make teaching word families easier and learning more fun, I've included tons of exciting learning activities that invite your students to identify word patterns, determine nonsense words, and build essential phonics skills. You'll find hands-on learning activities such as the Word Family Activity Mats, Concentration game boards, and Word Work game boards. Plus, I've included easy-to-use reproducible templates for Bingo, Word Wheels, Flash Cards, Flip Books, Toss-a-Word, and more. Many of the reproducibles in this book are terrific for interactive homework, small group lessons, and learning centers. It's easy to weave the games and activities in this book into your reading program. Every learning activity is fun and ready to use.

How to Use This Book

Using Word Family Activity Mats

Activity mats are a great way to introduce kids to working with word families. Each is filled with delightful opportunities for children to read and write many words within each word family. As students learn one word family pattern, they begin to read at least ten other words. To make instruction even easier, you'll find a word family activity mat for each of the word families presented in this book. Each mat focuses instruction on ten words within each word family that students will frequently encounter as they read and write. As you plan your lessons, use the grid one page 5 to locate specific words covered in this book. Whether you have your students complete the activity mats in your learning centers or as fun-to-do homework, they're sure to be a hit!

When you first introduce Word Family Activity Mats to your students, complete a few of the activity mats together as a class activity. Explain that each activity mat is made up of four learning activities. Three of the activities are: writing, reading, and alphabetizing. The fourth activity consists of different types of learning opportunities, including decoding puzzles, sentence fill-ins, word searches, and more. Each activity mat invites your students to:

◆ Read the ten word family words that appear at the top of each mat and write the letters of each word on the space below.

◆ Read the mini-story. Note how the word-family words fit within the context of a story.

◆ Circle each of the word-family words that appears in the story.

◆ Use scissors to cut out the words at the bottom. Then, glue the words in alphabetical order in the ABC Box on the right-hand side of the page. If you like, use the words with the Sort-the-Words activity on page 93.

◆ Complete the last activity, following the directions that have been provided.

Word Families Covered in This Book

Word Family Activity Mats	Phonogram	Words Included	Page
Short Vowels	-ab	cab, crab, dab, gab, grab, jab, lab, nab, scab, tab	7
	-ad	bad, Chad, dad, glad, had, lad, mad, pad, sad, tad	8
	-ag	bag, drag, flag, gag, nag, rag, sag, snag, tag, wag	9
	-am	clam, gram, ham, jam, Pam, ram, Sam, slam, swam, yam	10
	-an	can, Dan, fan, man, pan, plan, ran, tan, than, van	11
	-ap	cap, clap, flap, lap, map, nap, slap, snap, tap, trap	12
	-at	bat, cat, chat, fat, hat, mat, pat, rat, sat, that	13
	-ed	bed, fed, Fred, led, Ned, red, shed, sled, ted	14
	-ell	bell, fell, Nell, sell, shell, smell, spell, tell, well, yell	15
	-en	Ben, den, hen, Jen, men, pen, ten, then, when, yen	16
	-et	bet, get, jet, let, met, net, pet, set, wet, yet	17
	-id	bid, did, grid, hid, kid, lid, mid, rid, skid, slid	18
	-ig	big, dig, fig, gig, jig, pig, rig, sprig, twig, wig	19
	-ill	Bill, dill, fill, hill, ill, mill, pill, spill, still, will	20
	-in	bin, chin, grin, in, shin, skin, spin, thin, twin, win	21
	-ip	dip, flip, hip, lip, nip, ship, sip, skip, trip, zip	22
	-it	bit, fit, hit, it, kit, knit, lit, pit, quit, sit	23
	-og	bog, cog, clog, dog, fog, frog, hog, jog, log, smog	24
	-op	cop, drop, hop, mop, plop, pop, shop, slop, stop, top	25
	-ot	dot, cot, got, hot, knot, lot, not, pot, shot, spot	26
	-ug	bug, chug, dug, hug, lug, mug, rug, slug, snug, tug	27
	-um	strum, chum, drum, glum, gum, hum, yum, plum, sum, swum	28
	-ump	bump, clump, dump, grump, jump, lump, mump, pump, stump, thump	29
Consonant Blends (*ck, nk*)	-ack	back, black, jack, Mack, pack, rack, sack, snack, tack, track	30
	-ick	brick, chick, click, kick, lick, pick, sick, slick, stick, trick	31
	-ink	blink, drink, ink, kink, link, rink, sink, stink, think, wink	32
	-ock	block, clock, dock, knock, lock, rock, shock, smock, sock, tock	33
	-uck	buck, Chuck, cluck, duck, luck, pluck, puck, stuck, struck, truck	34
	-ank	bank, blank, drank, Frank, prank, rank, sank, spank, tank, yank	35
	-unk	bunk, chunk, dunk, drunk, hunk, junk, skunk, stunk, sunk, trunk	36
Consonant Digraphs (*sh*)	-ash	bash, cash, crash, dash, flash, hash, lash, rash, smash	37
Long Vowels (silent *e*)	-ake	bake, cake, flake, Jake, make, rake, shake, take, wake	38
	-ale	bale, gale, hale, male, pale, sale, scale, stale, tale, whale	39
	-ame	blame, came, fame, flame, frame, game, name, same, shame, tame	40
	-ate	crate, date, gate, grate, hate, Kate, late, plate, rate, skate	41
	-ice	dice, ice, lice, mice, nice, price, rice, slice, spice, twice	42
	-ide	bride, glide, hide, pride, ride, side, slide, stride, tide, wide	43
	-ine	dine, fine, line, mine, nine, pine, shine, tine, twine, vine	44
	-oke	broke, Coke, choke, joke, poke, smoke, spoke, stroke, woke, yoke	45
	-ore	chore, more, pore, score, shore, snore, sore, store, tore, wore	46
Vowel Digraphs (*ai, ea, aw*)	-ail	fail, Gail, mail, nail, pail, sail, snail, tail, trail, wail	47
	-ain	brain, chain, drain, grain, main, pain, plain, rain, Spain, train	48
	-eat	beat, cheat, cleat, eat, heat, meat, neat, seat, treat, wheat	49
	-aw	claw, draw, flaw, jaw, law, paw, raw, saw, slaw, straw	50
Controlled R	-ar	bar, car, far, jar, mar, par, scar, spar, star, tar	51
Endings (*ing, ay, est, y, ight*)	-ing	bring, king, ring, sing, spring, sting, string, swing, thing, wing	52
	-ay	day, gray, hay, jay, lay, may, play, say, stay, way	53
	-est	best, chest, crest, guest, nest, pest, rest, test, vest, west	54
	-y	by, cry, dry, fly, fry, my, shy, sty, try, why	55
	-ight	bright, fight, fright, knight, light, might, night, right, sight, tight	56

Helpful Hints

Learning word families and having fun go hand in hand when you use the games and activities in this book. The following suggestions will help make teaching word families easier to manage and easier to adapt to your students needs:

◆ Copy the game boards, cards, and other learning activities on a photocopier. Increasing the size of the reproducibles will make them easier for children to read and manipulate. Copying them onto cardboard will make them sturdier. Consider laminating game boards after the children have colored them, helping to ensure the game boards will be fun-to-use learning tools for years to come.

◆ Tuck word family games such as Word Work, Concentration, Toss-a-Word, Spin-the-Wheels, Word Family Dice, and Bingo in your classroom's writing center, making them accessible to kids. Remember, the more opportunities your students have to practice their developing knowledge of word families the better.

◆ Provide your students with opportunities to study word patterns independently. The reproducible Word Wheels, Slide-Throughs, Flip-Books, and Puzzles are great for independent work in the classroom. Ask your students to practice word patterns as a warm-up activity before a lesson, as a follow-up when they're done with their other work, and so on. You're sure to find lots of ways to incorporate the activities in this book with your curriculum.

◆ Support the school-home connection by sending games and activities home with your students. Invite them to teach their families how to play and share what they've learned. The Word Wheels, Slide-Throughs, Flip-Books, and Flashcards are portable and can be used by students most anywhere, including bus rides, plane trips, vacations—even the living room sofa!

Check Out These Super Sites!

National Council of Teachers of English: Why Talk About Phonics?
http://ncte.org/teach/Butler21575.html

Groff, Dr. Patrick. The Essence of Phonics.
http://www.nrrf.org/32_essence_of.html

The Order of Lessons. Phonics Tutor.
http://www.phonicstutor.com/orderoflessons.html

The Riggs Institute's Writing and Spelling Road to Reading and Thinking
http://www.riggsinst.org/index.html

Name _____ The _ab Family

cab	crab	dab	grab	lab
_ _ _	_ _ _ _	_ _ _	_ _ _ _	_ _ _
jab	nab	scab	tab	gab
_ _ _	_ _ _	_ _ _ _	_ _ _	_ _ _

Read the story. Circle all of the words that belong in the family.

ABC Box

1

Dab is a crab.

2

Dab is in the cab.

3

Dab is going to the lab.

4

Dab likes to grab.

Decode each word.

a	b	c	g

r	s	t

Cut the words apart. Put them in alphabetical order. Then glue them in the ABC Box.

cab	crab	dab	grab	lab
jab	nab	scab	tab	gab

7

Name_____

bad	Chad	dad	glad	had
_ _ _	_ _ _ _	_ _ _	_ _ _ _	_ _ _
lad	mad	pad	sad	tad
_ _ _	_ _ _	_ _ _	_ _ _	_ _ _

Read the story. Circle all of the words that belong in the family.

ABC Box

1

Chad is not glad.

2

I will not talk in cla...
I will not ta...

Chad has had a bad day.

3

Chad is a tad sad.

4

Poor Chad.

Answer each question.

1. What makes you sad? _____

_____

2. What makes you glad? _____

_____

Cut the words apart. Put them in alphabetical order. Then glue them in the ABC Box.

lad	pad	dad	tad	glad
had	Chad	bad	sad	mad

Name _____   The _ag Family

bag	drag	flag	gag	nag
---	----	----	---	---
rag	sag	snag	tag	wag
---	---	----	---	---

Read the story. Circle all of the words that belong in the family.

ABC Box

1 Wave the flag.

2 Cut the tag.

3 Carry the bag.

4 Feed the nag.

Write the word with the same meaning.

1. a sack: _____

2. a small towel: _____

3. an old horse: _____

4. a pennant: _____

5. a label: _____

6. to droop: _____

Cut the words apart. Put them in alphabetical order. Then glue them in the ABC Box.

bag	rag	flag	gag	wag
snag	tag	nag	drag	sag

9

clam	gram	ham	jam	Pam
____	____	___	___	___
ram	Sam	slam	swam	yam
___	___	____	____	___

Read the story. Circle all of the words that belong in the family.	ABC Box

1

Sam is a clam.

2

Sam weighs about a gram.

3

Sam likes to eat jam and ham.

4

Sam is the same size as a yam.

Use a red crayon to color the words. Use a blue crayon to color all the x's and z's to find the hidden words.

S	L	A	M	Z	X	Z	X	S	W	A	M
R	A	M	X	Z	X	G	R	A	M	Z	X
X	Z	X	Z	X	Z	X	Z	X	Y	A	M
Z	X	Z	X	H	A	M	Z	X	Z	X	Z
X	Z	X	Z	C	L	A	M	Z	X	Z	X
X	Z	X	Z	X	Z	X	Z	P	A	M	X
Z	X	Z	X	Z	X	S	A	M	Z	X	Z
J	A	M	X	Z	X	Z	X	Z	X	Z	X

Cut the words apart. Put them in alphabetical order. Then glue them in the ABC Box.

gram	Pam	clam	swam	yam
jam	Sam	slam	ram	ham

can	Dan	fan	man	pan
___	___	___	___	___
plan	ran	tan	than	van
____	___	___	____	___

Read the story. Circle all of the words that belong in the family.

ABC Box

1

Dan has a van.

2

Dan has a pan. He put the pan in the van.

3

Dan has a fan. He put the fan in the van.

4

Dan has a can. He put the can in the van.

Unscramble each word. Write it correctly on the line.

1. nar: _____

4. naf: _____

2. hatn: _____

5. nta: _____

3. pnal: _____

6. nap: _____

Cut the words apart. Put them in alphabetical order. Then glue them in the ABC Box.

man	Dan	van	than	pan
tan	can	ran	fan	plan

cap	clap	flap	lap	map
_ _ _	_ _ _ _	_ _ _ _	_ _ _	_ _ _
nap	slap	snap	tap	trap
_ _ _	_ _ _ _	_ _ _ _	_ _ _	_ _ _ _

Read the story. Circle all of the words that belong in the family.

ABC Box

1 I can clap my hands.

2 I can snap my fingers.

3 I can flap my arms.

4 I can tap my toes.

Decode each word.

a	c	l	p

r	s	t

_ _ _ _

_ _ _ _

Cut the words apart. Put them in alphabetical order. Then glue them in the ABC Box.

clap	lap	trap	tap	map
flap	snap	slap	cap	nap

Name _____

bat	cat	chat	fat	hat
_ _ _	_ _ _	_ _ _ _	_ _ _	_ _ _
mat	pat	rat	sat	that
_ _ _	_ _ _	_ _ _	_ _ _	_ _ _ _

Read the story. Circle all of the words that belong in the family.

ABC Box

1

The fat cat knows a rat.

2

That rat sat on a mat.

3

The bat came to chat with the cat and the rat.

4

The bat has a hat.

Write the missing letter.

h_ _t   ma_   t_ _at   c_ _at   fa_

c_ _t   ra_   s_ _t   b_ _t   pa_

Cut the words apart. Put them in alphabetical order. Then glue them in the ABC Box.

hat	chat	cat	rat	sat
bat	pat	that	fat	mat

bed	fed	Fred	led	Ned
---	---	----	---	---

red	shed	sled	ted	wed
---	----	----	---	---

Read the story. Circle all of the words that belong in the family.

ABC Box

1 This is Ned. Ned has a ted.

2 This is Ned and his ted Fred.

3 Fred is on Ned's bed.

4 Fred is on Ned's sled.

Color Fred.

Cut the words apart. Put them in alphabetical order. Then glue them in the ABC Box.

ted	red	Ned	Fred	sled
led	shed	fed	wed	bed

bell	fell	Nell	sell	shell
____	____	____	____	_____
smell	spell	tell	well	yell
_____	_____	____	____	____

Read the story. Circle all of the words that belong in the family.

ABC Box

1 This is Nell.
Nell is by a well.

2 Nell has a shell.

3 The shell smells.

4 A snail is in the shell.
Nell yells!

Decode each word.

a	d	e	i	k
l	n	o	s	t

____ ____ ____

____ ____ ____

Cut the words apart. Put them in alphabetical order. Then glue them in the ABC Box.

well	fell	Nell	tell	smell
sell	shell	bell	yell	spell

Name _____

Ben	den	hen	Jen	men
___	___	___	___	___
pen	ten	then	when	yen
___	___	____	____	___

Read the story. Circle all of the words that belong in the family.

ABC Box

1

Ben has a hen.

2

The hen's name is Jen.

3

Jen the hen lives in a pen.

4

The pen was made by ten men.

Write a question for Ben about his hen.
Make sure the question begins with "when."

_____

_____

Word Power! Write the word that means
"something to write with" and a "place to keep an animal." _____

Cut the words apart. Put them in alphabetical order. Then glue them in the ABC Box.

hen	yen	Jen	pen	men
when	den	then	ten	Ben

Name _____

bet	get	jet	let	met
---	---	---	---	---
net	pet	set	wet	yet
---	---	---	---	---

Read the story. Circle all of the words that belong in the family.

ABC Box

1 Have you met Chet, yet?

2 Chet is my pet.

3 Chet likes to get wet.

4 Chet likes to ride in my jet.

Find and color each word in the word search.

B	N	E	T	C	N	Y	E	T	L	C	G
X	G	D	D	Y	C	B	B	I	M	E	T
X	K	L	Y	P	E	T	V	N	V	S	K
L	E	T	G	A	N	J	E	T	Y	K	G
P	G	R	Y	L	B	E	T	X	A	Y	P
W	E	T	U	O	D	G	E	T	F	J	A
K	C	R	W	B	V	R	S	E	T	R	U
N	R	D	R	S	U	A	W	Q	S	C	O

Cut the words apart. Put them in alphabetical order. Then glue them in the ABC Box.

wet	bet	set	yet	pet
met	net	let	jet	get

bid	did	grid	hid	kid
___	___	____	___	___
lid	mid	rid	skid	slid
___	___	___	____	____

Read the story. Circle all of the words that belong in the family.

ABC Box

1

Who slid? The kid did.

2

Who hid? The kid did.

3

Who skid? The kid did.

4

Who bid? The kid did.

Find and color each word in the word search.

G	R	I	D	N	S	K	I	D	D	Y	D
S	L	I	D	X	S	R	I	D	H	L	B
Z	R	D	W	V	P	E	E	V	K	I	D
M	E	N	T	B	I	D	K	H	O	R	T
M	I	D	S	M	D	J	V	L	I	D	A
N	R	L	C	Y	X	O	I	M	J	W	I
L	H	Z	H	T	O	D	I	D	F	T	V
H	I	D	K	N	X	A	Z	O	B	N	F

Cut the words apart. Put them in alphabetical order. Then glue them in the ABC Box.

grid	hid	rid	bid	lid
mid	kid	slid	did	skid

Name _____   The _ig Family

big	dig	fig	gig	jig

pig	rig	sprig	twig	wig
---	---	-----	----	---

Read the story. Circle all of the words that belong in the family.   ABC Box

1

The big pig has a wig.

2

The big pig has a fig.

3

The big pig has a rig.

4

The big pig has a twig.

Complete each sentence.

1. A _____ is a kind of fruit.

2. A small branch is a _____ .

3. A shovel is used to _____ .

4. A _____ is a dance.

5. A _____ is fake hair.

6. A giant is _____ .

Cut the words apart. Put them in alphabetical order. Then glue them in the ABC Box.

sprig	fig	twig	dig	wig
rig	pig	gig	jig	big

Name _____   The _ill Family

Bill	dill	fill	hill	ill
____	____	____	____	___
mill	pill	spill	still	will
____	____	_____	_____	____

Read the story. Circle all of the words that belong in the family.   ABC Box

1

This is Bill.

2

Bill went to the mill.

3

The mill is on the hill.

4

Bill will fill the pail.
Bill will not let it spill.

ACROSS
3. to knock over
5. sick
6. to load

DOWN
1. a pickle
2. a name
3. not moving
4. small mountain

Cut the words apart. Put them in alphabetical order. Then glue them in the ABC Box.

ill	Bill	mill	still	spill
fill	pill	dill	hill	will

20

bin	chin	grin	in	shin
___	____	____	__	____
skin	spin	thin	twin	win
____	____	____	____	___

Read the story. Circle all of the words that belong in the family.   ABC Box

1

I have a chin.

2

I have a big grin.

3

I have a lot of skin.

4

I have a twin.

Decode each word.

c	g	h	i

n	r	s

___ ___ ___

___ ___ ___

___ ___ ___

___ ___

Cut the words apart. Put them in alphabetical order. Then glue them in the ABC Box.

grin	chin	skin	twin	bin
in	win	spin	thin	shin

dip	flip	hip	lip	nip
___	____	___	___	___
ship	sip	skip	trip	zip
____	___	____	____	___

Read the story. Circle all of the words that belong in the family.

ABC Box

1 Skip can take a dip.

2 Skip can do a back flip.

3 Skip can bend at the hip.

4 Skip is very hip!

Write each word next to its meaning.

1. a small bite: _____

2. a small drink: _____

3. a big boat: _____

4. not a walk nor a run: _____

5. to fall or a vacation: _____

6. to move fast: _____

Cut the words apart. Put them in alphabetical order. Then glue them in the ABC Box.

dip	skip	sip	flip	hip
ship	trip	zip	nip	lip

Name _____ The _it Family

bit	fit	hit	it	kit
---	---	---	--	---

knit	lit	pit	quit	sit
----	---	---	----	---

Read the story. Circle all of the words that belong in the family. | ABC Box

①

I have a kit.

②

With the kit, I will sit.

③

I will knit for a bit.

④

I will not quit until it is a good fit.

Write each misspelled word correctly on the line.

Example: pite: pit   3. et: _____

1. knet: _____   4. kwit: _____

2. biit: _____   5. figt: _____

Cut the words apart. Put them in alphabetical order. Then glue them in the ABC Box.

it	pit	quit	kit	sit
bit	fit	spit	knit	lit

Name _____ The _og Family

bog	cog	clog	dog	fog
---	---	----	---	---

frog	hog	jog	log	smog
----	---	---	---	----

Read the story. Circle all of the words that belong in the family.

ABC Box

① The frog is lost in the fog.

② The dog is lost in the fog.

③ The hog is lost in the fog.

④ They all meet at the log in the bog.

Write the missing letters to complete the crossword puzzle.

Cut the words apart. Put them in alphabetical order. Then glue them in the ABC Box.

cog	log	fog	bog	dog
clog	hog	frog	jog	smog

24

Name _____

cop	drop	hop	mop	plop
___	____	___	___	____
pop	shop	slop	stop	top
___	____	____	____	___

Read the story. Circle all of the words that belong in the family.

ABC Box

1 Flop likes to hop.

2 Flop likes soda pop.

3 Flop likes to shop.

4 Flop likes to mop.

Write a sentence telling about something you like to do. Draw a picture to go with your sentence.

_____

_____

_____

_____

Cut the words apart. Put them in alphabetical order. Then glue them in the ABC Box.

top	shop	hop	slop	cop
drop	pop	plop	stop	mop

Name _____

cot	dot	got	hot	knot
– – –	– – –	– – –	– – –	– – – –
lot	not	pot	shot	spot
– – –	– – –	– – –	– – – –	– – – –

Read the story. Circle all of the words that belong in the family.

ABC Box

1

This is a pot.

2

This is a knot.

3

This is a cot.

4

This is a dot.

Write each word next to its meaning.

1. unable to: _____

2. a little bed: _____

3. not cold: _____

4. a pan: _____

5. a place: _____

Cut the words apart. Put them in alphabetical order. Then glue them in the ABC Box.

pot	dot	shot	spot	knot
got	cot	not	hot	lot

bug	chug	dug	hug	lug
---	----	---	---	---

mug	rug	slug	snug	tug
---	---	----	----	---

Read the story. Circle all of the words that belong in the family.

ABC Box

1 Do you see the bug?

2 Do you see the slug?

3 The slug is on the rug.

4 The bug has a mug.

Find and color each word in the word search.

D	U	G	B	S	N	H	U	G	D	Y	D
S	L	U	G	X	S	H	R	U	G	L	B
Z	R	D	M	U	G	W	V	S	N	U	G
L	U	G	P	E	E	V	C	H	U	G	M
E	N	T	K	H	O	R	T	B	U	G	S
T	U	G	M	D	J	V	A	N	R	L	C

Cut the words apart. Put them in alphabetical order. Then glue them in the ABC Box.

slug	mug	hug	chug	dug
snug	tug	bug	rug	lug

strum	chum	drum	glum	gum
_ _ _ _ _	_ _ _ _	_ _ _ _	_ _ _ _	_ _ _
hum	yum	plum	sum	swum
_ _ _	_ _ _	_ _ _ _	_ _ _	_ _ _ _

Read the story. Circle all of the words that belong in the family.

ABC Box

1

My chum felt glum.

2

So I gave my chum a plum and gum.

3

He said, "Yum!" and began to hum and strum.

4

I played my drum.

Write the word with the same meaning.

1. math answer: _____

2. sad: _____

3. pal: _____

4. fruit: _____

Cut the words apart. Put them in alphabetical order. Then glue them in the ABC Box.

plum	glum	drum	hum	sum
yum	gum	chum	strum	swum

Name _____ The _ump Family

bump	clump	dump	grump	jump
_ _ _ _	_ _ _ _ _	_ _ _ _	_ _ _ _ _	_ _ _ _
lump	mump	pump	stump	thump
_ _ _ _	_ _ _ _	_ _ _ _	_ _ _ _ _	_ _ _ _ _

Read the story. Circle all of the words that belong in the family.

ABC Box

1 Stan is a grump.

2 Stan has the mumps.

3 Stan's mumps are red lumps.

4 Stan is down in the dumps.

Unscramble each word. Write it correctly on the line.

1. pclum: _____

2. pdum: _____

3. pstum: _____

4. pthum: _____

Cut the words apart. Put them in alphabetical order. Then glue them in the ABC Box.

pump	jump	lump	bump	mump
clump	dump	thump	stump	grump

Name _____ The _ack Family

back	black	jack	Mack	pack
____	_____	____	____	____
rack	sack	snack	tack	track
____	____	_____	____	_____

Read the story. Circle all of the words that belong in the family.

ABC Box

1

Mack has a black backpack.

2

Jack has a backpack, too.

3

Mack put his backpack on his back.

4

Mack's snack is in the pack.

Complete each compound word.

thumb_____

back_____

flap_____

Cut the words apart. Put them in alphabetical order. Then glue them in the ABC Box.

tack	pack	track	Mack	snack
jack	black	back	sack	rack

30

Name _____   The _ick Family

brick	chick	click	kick	lick
_ _ _ _ _	_ _ _ _ _	_ _ _ _ _	_ _ _ _	_ _ _ _
pick	sick	slick	stick	trick
_ _ _ _	_ _ _ _	_ _ _ _ _	_ _ _ _ _	_ _ _ _ _

Read the story. Circle all of the words that belong in the family.

ABC Box

1 Nick is a chick.

2 Nick builds with bricks.

3 He builds with sticks.

4 Nick likes his house of sticks and bricks.

Write three other words that belong in this family.

_____   _____

Word Power!
Travis fell on the slick sidewalk. Why would a sidewalk be called "slick"? Explain.

_____

_____

Cut the words apart. Put them in alphabetical order. Then glue them in the ABC Box.

brick	click	stick	pick	trick
slick	sick	lick	kick	chick

blink	drink	ink	kink	link
_ _ _ _ _	_ _ _ _ _	_ _ _	_ _ _ _	_ _ _ _
rink	sink	stink	think	wink
_ _ _ _	_ _ _ _	_ _ _ _ _	_ _ _ _ _	_ _ _ _

Read the story. Circle all of the words that belong in the family.

ABC Box

1

The snake is in a kink.

2

The pig is nice and pink.

3

The hen is in the sink.

4

The skunk stinks!

Use the red crayon to color all of the words in the word search. Use a blue crayon to color all of the remaining x's to find the hidden words.

X	L	I	N	K	X	S	T	I	N	K	X
T	H	I	N	K	X	X	X	X	X	X	X
X	X	X	X	X	B	L	I	N	K	X	X
X	X	X	X	X	S	I	N	K	X	X	X
D	R	I	N	K	X	X	X	X	X	X	X
W	I	N	K	X	X	S	I	N	K	X	X
R	I	N	K	X	X	X	X	X	X	X	X
X	X	X	X	X	X	X	K	I	N	K	X

Cut the words apart. Put them in alphabetical order. Then glue them in the ABC Box.

ink	sink	drink	rink	stink
link	blink	kink	think	wink

32

block	clock	dock	knock	lock
_ _ _ _ _	_ _ _ _ _	_ _ _ _	_ _ _ _ _	_ _ _ _
rock	shock	smock	sock	tock
_ _ _ _	_ _ _ _ _	_ _ _ _ _	_ _ _ _	_ _ _ _

Read the story. Circle all of the words that belong in the family.   ABC Box

1

I have a clock.

2

The clock looks like a block.

3

TICK TOCK   TICK TOCK

The clock says "tick tock."

4

RING RING

When it rings, it's a shock.

Complete the sentences.

1. I will _____ on the door.

2. He will play with the _____ .

3. Did you _____ the door.

4. I have an orange _____ .

5. The boat is by the _____ .

6. The _____ is gray and hard .

Cut the words apart. Put them in alphabetical order. Then glue them in the ABC Box.

sock	dock	block	shock	rock
tock	clock	knock	lock	smock

buck	Chuck	cluck	duck	luck
____	_____	_____	____	____
pluck	puck	stuck	struck	truck
_____	____	_____	_____	_____

Read the story. Circle all of the words that belong in the family.

ABC Box

1 This is Chuck.

2 Chuck has a truck.

3 The truck is stuck.

4 Chuck has bad luck.

Find and color each word in the word search.

C	H	U	C	K	B	A	X	D	U	C	K
B	U	C	K	C	L	U	C	K	H	H	P
R	V	S	L	U	C	K	S	T	U	C	K
S	T	R	U	C	K	M	P	U	C	K	F
P	L	U	C	K	T	M	L	Y	T	C	P
T	R	U	C	K	K	T	P	O	J	D	F

Cut the words apart. Put them in alphabetical order. Then glue them in the ABC Box.

Chuck	puck	truck	cluck	duck
pluck	buck	struck	luck	stuck

bank	blank	drank	Frank	prank
_____	_____	_____	_____	_____
rank	sank	spank	tank	yank
_____	_____	_____	_____	_____

Read the story. Circle all of the words that belong in the family.

ABC Box

1 Who sank the boat? Hank and Frank sank the boat.

2 Who drank the milk? Hank and Frank drank the milk.

3 Who filled the tank? Hank and Frank filled the tank.

4 Who went to the bank? Hank and Frank went to the bank.

Write three other words that belong in this family.

_____ _____ _____

Word Power!
Sam left his paper blank. What does the word "blank" mean in this sentence?

_____

_____

Cut the words apart. Put them in alphabetical order. Then glue them in the ABC Box.

yank	tank	prank	Frank	spank
drank	sank	blank	rank	bank

bunk	chunk	dunk	drunk	hunk
____	_____	____	_____	____
junk	skunk	stunk	sunk	trunk
____	_____	_____	____	_____

Read the story. Circle all of the words that belong in the family.

ABC Box

1

Look at all this junk!

2

I cannot see your bunk!

3

Put the toys in the trunk.

4

Now get in your bunk!

Write the word with the same meaning.

1. chest: _____

2. bed: _____

3. score a basket: _____

4. not floating: _____

5. a pile of stuff: _____

6. a big piece: _____

Cut the words apart. Put them in alphabetical order. Then glue them in the ABC Box.

sunk	chunk	bunk	dunk	junk
hunk	skunk	drunk	trunk	stunk

Name _____ The _ash Family

bash	cash	crash	dash	flash
____	____	_____	____	_____

hash	lash	rash	smash	trash
____	____	____	_____	_____

Read the story. Circle all of the words that belong in the family.

ABC Box

1. Ash has some cash.

2. Ash will dash to the store.

3. Ash will get some hash browns.

4. Ash will be back in a flash.

Unscramble each word. Write it correctly on the line.

1. shar: _____

2. shatr: _____

3. sabh: _____

4. achs: _____

5. achrs: _____

6. adsh: _____

Cut the words apart. Put them in alphabetical order. Then glue them in the ABC Box.

hash	flash	cash	bash	trash
rash	crash	dash	smash	lash

37

bake	cake	flake	Jake	make
____	____	_____	____	____
rake	shake	snake	take	wake
____	_____	_____	____	____

Read the story. Circle all of the words that belong in the family.

ABC Box

1

Jake will bake the cake.

2

Jake will wake the snake.

3

Jake will rake the flakes.

4

Jake will make the shake.

Write a sentence telling about a food you might like to bake. Draw a picture to go with your sentence.

_____

_____

_____

Cut the words apart. Put them in alphabetical order. Then glue them in the ABC Box.

wake	snake	Jake	make	cake
flake	rake	bake	shake	take

bale	gale	hale	male	pale
____	____	____	____	____
sale	scale	stale	tale	whale
_____	_____	_____	____	_____

Read the story. Circle all of the words that belong in the family.

ABC Box

1 The whale is on the scale.

2 The whale is a male.

3 The whale is pale.

4 The whale bought a ball on sale.

Write the missing letter.

s__le   tal__   s__ale   st__le

w__ale   pa__e   g__le   mal__

Cut the words apart. Put them in alphabetical order. Then glue them in the ABC Box.

bale	male	scale	sale	pale
gale	whale	tale	hale	stale

blame	came	fame	flame	frame
_ _ _ _ _	_ _ _ _	_ _ _ _	_ _ _ _ _	_ _ _ _ _
game	name	same	shame	tame
_ _ _ _	_ _ _ _	_ _ _ _	_ _ _ _ _	_ _ _ _

Read the story. Circle all of the words that belong in the family.

ABC Box

1 We have the same games.

2 We have the same names.

3 We have the same frames.

4 We are the same!

Draw a line matching the same words.

flame	came
shame	tame
fame	flame
tame	shame
lame	fame
came	lame

Cut the words apart. Put them in alphabetical order. Then glue them in the ABC Box.

flame	shame	frame	same	game
fame	name	came	tame	blame

Name _____

crate	date	gate	grate	hate
_ _ _ _ _	_ _ _ _	_ _ _ _	_ _ _ _ _	_ _ _ _
Kate	late	plate	rate	skate
_ _ _ _	_ _ _ _	_ _ _ _ _	_ _ _ _	_ _ _ _ _

Read the story. Circle all of the words that belong in the family.   ABC Box

① Kate has ice skates.

② Kate will skate to the gate.

③ Kate will pick up the crate.

④ Kate will put a plate on the crate.

Complete the sentences.

1. Kate will _____ to the _____ .

2. The _____ is on the crate.

3. The _____ is heavy.

4. _____ is a girl.

5. A _____ is a fruit.

6. Kate is never _____ .

Cut the words apart. Put them in alphabetical order. Then glue them in the ABC Box.

crate	date	plate	late	skate
hate	Kate	grate	gate	rate

dice	ice	lice	mice	nice
____	___	____	____	____
price	rice	slice	spice	twice
_____	____	_____	_____	_____

Read the story. Circle all of the words that belong in the family.

ABC Box

1

The mice had a bite of cheese.

2

The mice had a bite of rice.

3

The mice had a bite of ice.

4

The mice had a bite of spice.

Write the answer to each riddle.

1. I melt when its hot. _____

2. We love to eat cheese. _____

3. I have dots on all sides. _____

4. I tell how much something costs. _____

5. I did it two times. _____

Cut the words apart. Put them in alphabetical order. Then glue them in the ABC Box.

slice	ice	price	lice	rice
nice	mice	twice	dice	spice

bride	glide	hide	pride	ride
_ _ _ _ _	_ _ _ _ _	_ _ _ _	_ _ _ _ _	_ _ _ _
side	slide	stride	tide	wide
_ _ _ _	_ _ _ _ _	_ _ _ _ _ _	_ _ _ _	_ _ _ _

Read the story. Circle all of the words that belong in the family.   ABC Box

1 Let's go outside.

2 We can go on the slide.

3 The slide is wide.

4 It is fun to glide down the slide.

Unscramble each word. Write it correctly on the line.

1. idebr: _____

2. sdie: _____

3. iwde: _____

4. hdei: _____

5. gilde: _____

6. pidre: _____

Cut the words apart. Put them in alphabetical order. Then glue them in the ABC Box.

slide	ride	pride	wide	glide
stride	bride	side	tide	hide

dine	fine	line	mine	nine
____	____	____	____	____

pine	shine	tine	twine	vine
____	_____	____	_____	____

Read the story. Circle all of the words that belong in the family.

ABC Box

1

I see a ball of twine.

2

I see a vine.

3

I see a fork with tines.

4

I see a sun that shines.

Complete each sentences.

1. I will use _____ to tie the box.

2. The _____ grows on a trellis.

3. Cats have _____ lives.

4. We will _____ at the restaurant.

5. You will _____ your shoes.

6. The toys are all _____ !

Cut the words apart. Put them in alphabetical order. Then glue them in the ABC Box.

dine	pine	shine	mine	nine
tine	twine	fine	line	vine

Name _____ The _oke Family

broke	Coke	choke	joke	poke
_ _ _ _ _	_ _ _ _	_ _ _ _ _	_ _ _ _	_ _ _ _
smoke	spoke	stroke	woke	yoke
_ _ _ _ _	_ _ _ _ _	_ _ _ _ _	_ _ _ _	_ _ _ _

Read the story. Circle all of the words that belong in the family.

ABC Box

① Pam woke up one day.

② She broke her clock.

③ Then Pam spoke.

④ "This is not a funny joke!"

Find and color the words in the word search.

B	R	O	K	E	E	R	W	O	K	E	M
S	M	O	K	E	B	C	O	K	E	S	N
J	O	K	E	D	Y	D	X	S	H	L	B
Z	R	D	W	V	P	S	T	R	O	K	E
C	H	O	K	E	E	E	V	M	E	N	T
K	H	O	R	T	S	M	D	J	V	A	N
R	L	C	Y	X	O	P	O	K	E	I	M
S	P	O	K	E	J	W	Y	O	K	E	I

Cut the words apart. Put them in alphabetical order. Then glue them in the ABC Box.

Coke	choke	joke	poke	woke
yoke	broke	stroke	smoke	spoke

chore	more	pore	score	shore
_ _ _ _ _	_ _ _ _	_ _ _ _	_ _ _ _ _	_ _ _ _ _
snore	sore	store	tore	wore
_ _ _ _ _	_ _ _ _	_ _ _ _ _	_ _ _ _	_ _ _ _

Read the story. Circle all of the words that belong in the family.

ABC Box

1 I did my chores.

2 I went to the store.

3 I went to the shore.

4 Now I am sore!

Write the word with the same meaning.

1. beach: _____

2. job: _____

3. to ache: _____

Draw a picture of the chore you do at your house.

Cut the words apart. Put them in alphabetical order. Then glue them in the ABC Box.

score	store	more	snore	chore
shore	sore	pore	tore	wore

fail	Gail	mail	nail	pail
____	____	____	____	____
sail	snail	tail	trail	wail
____	_____	____	_____	____

Read the story. Circle all of the words that belong in the family.

ABC Box

1 Gail has a pet snail. When the snail goes with Gail, it leaves a trail.

2 Gail goes to get the mail. The snail leaves a trail.

3 Gail goes to get a pail. The snail leaves a trail.

4 Gail goes to get the nail. The snail leaves a trail.

Would you like to have a pet snail? Why or why not?

_____

_____

_____

Cut the words apart. Put them in alphabetical order. Then glue them in the ABC Box.

nail	Gail	mail	snail	sail
wail	tail	fail	pail	trail

Name _____

brain	chain	drain	grain	main
_ _ _ _ _	_ _ _ _ _	_ _ _ _ _	_ _ _ _ _	_ _ _ _
pain	plain	rain	Spain	train
_ _ _ _	_ _ _ _ _	_ _ _ _	_ _ _ _ _	_ _ _ _ _

Read the story. Circle all of the words that belong in the family.

ABC Box

1 I have a train.

2 The train is from Spain.

SPAIN

3 The train is plain.

4 It carries chain and grain.

Complete each sentence.

Your _____ is in your head.

A _____ rides on a track.

Oats are a kind of _____ .

Water goes down the _____ in your sink.

Cut the words apart. Put them in alphabetical order. Then glue them in the ABC Box.

drain	brain	rain	chain	train
pain	Spain	plain	grain	main

48

Name _____   The _eat Family

beat	cheat	cleat	eat	heat
_ _ _ _	_ _ _ _ _	_ _ _ _ _	_ _ _	_ _ _ _
meat	neat	seat	treat	wheat
_ _ _ _	_ _ _ _	_ _ _ _	_ _ _ _ _	_ _ _ _ _

Read the story. Circle all of the words that belong in the family.

ABC Box

1

Have a seat.

2

We will have a treat.

3

The treat is not made of wheat.

4

We will eat the treat.

Write the word with the same meaning.

1. to win: _____

2. to be tidy: _____

3. a snack: _____

4. to warm up: _____

5. a grain: _____

6. where you sit: _____

Cut the words apart. Put them in alphabetical order. Then glue them in the ABC Box.

seat	heat	cleat	beat	treat
cheat	neat	meat	eat	wheat

claw	draw	flaw	jaw	law
____	____	____	___	___
paw	raw	saw	slaw	straw
___	___	___	____	_____

Read the story. Circle all of the words that belong in the family.

ABC Box

1
I have a big paw. What am I?

2
I have a big jaw. What am I?

3
I have a big claw. What am I?

4
I have a big straw. What am I?

Draw a picture of your favorite animal.

Cut the words apart. Put them in alphabetical order. Then glue them in the ABC Box.

paw	claw	saw	flaw	jaw
raw	draw	law	straw	slaw

bar	car	far	jar	mar
– – –	– – –	– – –	– – –	– – –
par	scar	spar	star	tar
– – –	– – – –	– – – –	– – – –	– – –

Read the story. Circle all of the words that belong in the family.	ABC Box

1

I have a big green jar.

2

I have a gold star.
I keep it in my big green jar.

3

I have a chocolate bar.
I keep it in my big green jar.

4

I have a red toy car.
I keep it in my big green jar.

How many words can you make using the letters in "CHOCOLATE BAR"?

1. _____   6. _____
2. _____   7. _____
3. _____   8. _____
4. _____   9. _____
5. _____   10. _____

Cut the words apart. Put them in alphabetical order. Then glue them in the ABC Box.

star	bar	scar	spar	tar
par	jar	mar	car	far

bring	king	ring	sing	spring
_ _ _ _ _	_ _ _ _	_ _ _ _	_ _ _ _	_ _ _ _ _ _
sting	string	swing	thing	wing
_ _ _ _ _	_ _ _ _ _ _	_ _ _ _ _	_ _ _ _ _	_ _ _ _

Read the story. Circle all of the words that belong in the family.

ABC Box

1 It is spring.

2 The bee will sting.

3 The king will sing.

4 And I will swing.

Complete each sentence.

1. I _____ my lunch to school in a lunch box.

2. Do you _____ in a choir?

3. My mother wears a gold _____ .

4. The queen and the _____ live in the castle.

Cut the words apart. Put them in alphabetical order. Then glue them in the ABC Box.

spring	wing	ring	thing	king
sting	sing	bring	string	swing

day	gray	hay	jay	lay
---	----	---	---	---
may	play	say	stay	way
---	----	---	----	---

Read the story. Circle all of the words that belong in the family.

ABC Box

1 The horse will eat the hay.

2 The pig will play.

3 The jay will sing all day.

4 The hen will lay the eggs.

Complete each sentence.

1. The blue _____ likes to sing.

2. The _____ horse is in the barn.

3. Do you know the _____ to my house?

4. Would you like to _____ marbles?

Cut the words apart. Put them in alphabetical order. Then glue them in the ABC Box.

way	may	jay	play	say
hay	lay	stay	gray	day

Name _____   The _est Family

best	chest	crest	guest	nest
----	-----	-----	-----	----
pest	rest	test	vest	west
----	----	----	----	----

Read the story. Circle all of the words that belong in the family.   ABC Box

1. I made a nest.

2. I did my best.

3. It has a guest.

4. The guest is in the nest.

Complete each sentence.

1. My little brother can be a real _____ .

2. Do you need to take a little _____ ?

3. Where did you find the treasure _____ ?

Cut the words apart. Put them in alphabetical order. Then glue them in the ABC Box.

nest	test	rest	west	crest
best	pest	guest	vest	chest

54

Name _____ The _y Family

by	cry	dry	fly	fry
– –	– – –	– – –	– – –	– – –
my	shy	sty	try	why
– –	– – –	– – –	– – –	– – –

Read the story. Circle all of the words that belong in the family.

1 Ty will fry the eggs.

2 Ty will dry the dishes.

3 Ty will clean the pig sty.

4 Ty will fly the plane.

Write three other words that belong in this family.

1. _____

2. _____

3. _____

Cut the words apart. Put them in alphabetical order. Then glue them in the ABC Box.

by	fly	try	shy	my
cry	sty	why	dry	fry

bright	fight	fright	knight	light
_____	_____	_____	_____	_____

might	night	right	sight	tight
_____	_____	_____	_____	_____

Read the story. Circle all of the words that belong in the family.

ABC Box

1 Last night, I saw a knight.

2 The knight was under a light.

3 The knight was shiny bright.

4 The knight was quite a sight!

Use a red crayon to color the words. Use a blue crayon to color all the x's, y's, and z's to discover the hidden words.

N	I	G	H	T	B	R	I	G	H	T	X
X	Y	Z	X	M	I	G	H	T	X	X	Z
L	I	G	H	T	Z	T	I	G	H	T	X
R	I	G	H	T	Y	X	S	I	G	H	T
Y	Z	F	R	I	G	H	T	Z	Y	X	Z
K	N	I	G	H	T	X	N	Y	Z	X	Y
X	Y	Z	X	Y	Z	X	Y	Z	Y	X	Y
F	I	G	H	T	Z	Y	X	Y	Z	X	Y

Cut the words apart. Put them in alphabetical order. Then glue them in the ABC Box.

knight	tight	light	fright	night
fight	right	bright	might	sight

Word Work

Directions for Play

- Each pair of students will need one playing board and 20 counters (two colors, ten of each color).

- Cut apart the letter cards; shuffle and lay them in a stack facedown. Turn over the top card and the game is ready to begin.

- Taking turns, each student turns over one card. If the card can be used with one of the cards already turned over, the student may take the two cards and cover the matching picture with a counter. This student may take another turn. If the cards cannot be used to make a word, they are left faceup on the table and the other student may take his turn.

- If a student does not use a card that could have made a word, the other student may take the two cards and then take a turn.

- A student wins when markers form a row. The row may be on the horizontal or vertical. Older students may enjoy forming rows on the diagonal.

Extension Ideas

- After playing the game in class, students may take the game boards home and play the game with their families.

- The game boards can be colored, laminated, and placed at a center.

Word Work Answer Key

- **ab, ad, ag, am:** crab, yam, nag, ham, clam, lab, bag, sad, jam, tag, cab, flag

- **an, ap, at:** van, rat, cat, fan, clap, pan, hat, can, snap, tap, bat, Dan

- **ed, ell, en, et:** jet, pen, hen, well, men, pet, shell, ted, Ned, bed, smell, wet

- **id, ig, ill:** kid, pig, twig, bid, hill, fig, mill, rig, hid, skid, wig, slid

- **og, op, ot:** frog, pot, dog, dot, shop, fog, cot, pop, knot, hop, hog, log

- **ug, um, ump:** gum, grump, plum, drum, mug, slug, glum, bug, lump, rug, jump, yum

- **ock, uck, ank, unk, ash:** clock, cash, bank, tank, trunk, bunk, shock, sank, block, stuck, trunk, dash

- **ake, ale, ame, ate:** snake, gate, game, sale, whale, flake, skate, plate, Kate, crate, Jake, brake

- **ice, ide, ine, oke, ore:** broke, mice, rice, wide, vine, twine, slide, ice, shine, tine, spice, shore

- **ail, ain, eat, aw, ar:** pail, train, star, claw, car, jar, Spain, paw, eat, treat, snail, nail

- **ing, ay, est, y, ight:** wing, swing, light, jay, fry, night, spring, king, fly, dry, knight, nest

- **ack, ick, ink, in, ip, it:** brick, flip, chin, chick, hip, grin, tack, kink, knit, snack, stick, pack

Word Work

cl	cr	c	<u>n</u>
l	y	<u>b</u>	s
j	t	h	fl
__am	__am	__am	__am
__ab	__ab	__ab	__ad
__ag	__ag	__ag	__ag

Word Work

Word Families: an, ap, at

D	b	t	sn
cl	p	h	c
v	r	c	f
__at	__at	__at	__at
__ap	__ap	__ap	__an
__an	__an	__an	__an

Word Work

N	b	sm	w
m	p	sh	t
j	p	h	w
__en	__en	__en	__ell
__ell	__ell	__et	__et
__et	__ed	__ed	__ed

Word Work

Word Families: id, ig, ill

h	sk	<u>w</u>	sl
r	<u>m</u>	f	h
<u>b</u>	tw	p̲	k
_ig	_ig	_ig	_ig
_ig	_ill	_ill	_id
_id	_id	_id	_id

Word Work

Word Families: og, op, ot

f	kn	h	l
sh	h	c	d̲
fr	p̶	d̲	p̶
__op	__op	__op	__ot
__ot	__ot	__ot	__og
__og	__og	__og	__og

Word Work

Word Families: ug, um, ump

l	r	j	y
b	gl	sl	m
g	gr	pl	dr
__ump	__ump	__ump	__ug
__ug	__ug	__ug	__um
__um	__um	__um	__um

Word Work

Word Families: ock, uck, ank, unk, ash

d	tr	st	bl
s	sh	b	tr
cl	c	b	t
__uck	__uck	__unk	__unk
__ank	__ank	__ank	__ash
__ash	__ock	__ock	__ock

Word Work

Word Families: ake, ale, ame, ate

b	J	cr	K
pl	sk	fl	wh
s	g	g	sn
__ame	__ale	__ale	__ake
__ake	__ake	__ake	__ate
__ate	__ate	__ate	__ate

Word Work

Word Families: ice, ide, ine, oke, ore

sh	sp	t	sh
tw	r	w	br
(blank)	v	m	sl
__ide	__ide	__ore	__oke
__ice	__ice	__ice	__ice
__ine	__ine	__ine	__ine

Word Work

Word Families: ail, ain, eat, aw, ar

c	tr	cl	p
p	j	Sp	sn
(blank)	tr	st	<u>n</u>
__ar	__ar	__ar	__eat
__eat	__ail	__ail	__ail
__aw	__aw	__ain	__ain

Word Work

n	kn	dr	fl
fr	n	sp	k
j	l	sw	w
__ay	__ing	__ing	__ing
__ing	__est	__y	__y
__y	__ight	__ight	__ight

68

Word Work

Word Families: ack, ick, ink, in, ip, it

br	fl	ch	ch
h	gr	t	sn
k	kn	st	p
_ick	_ick	_ick	_it
_ip	_ip	_in	_in
_ink	_ack	_ack	_ack

Concentration Word Cards and Pictures are terrific for teaching word families. Whether they're playing Concentration or Nine Cards, your students are sure to have fun.

Concentration

Directions for Play

◆ Photocopy the picture cards and words onto construction paper or card stock. Cut the words and pictures apart and lay them facedown in a 3 x 4 card arrangement.

◆ Taking turns, each student turns over two cards. If the cards match, the student keeps both cards and gets to take another turn.

◆ If the cards do not match, the student turns over the cards again and another student takes a turn.

◆ Play continues until all of the cards have been paired. The student with the most pairs of cards wins the game.

Nine Cards

Directions for Play

◆ Photocopy 2 or 3 different sets of Concentration words and pictures onto construction paper or card stock. Cut the words and pictures apart. Shuffle the cards and place in a stack facedown.

◆ Lay nine cards out on a 3 x 3 arrangement (see below).

◆ The first player finds all words and pictures that match and removes them from the arrangement. (In the example, the player would take the smiling person picture and the word "grin"; the push pin picture and the word "tack".)

◆ Using the remaining cards, the first player fills in the four empty spaces. The second player takes her turn and removes all words and pictures that match.

◆ Continue in this manner until all of the cards have been used. The player with the most pairs wins the game.

	grin	tack
brick		
	snack	chick

Concentration

crab	yam	nag	ham
clam	lab	bag	sad
jam	tag	cab	flag

Concentration

Word Families: an, ap, at

van	rat	cat	fan
clap	pan	hat	can
snap	tap	bat	Dan

Concentration

jet	pen	hen	well
men	pet	shell	ted
Ned	bed	smell	wet

Concentration

kid	pig	twig	bid
hill	fig	mill	rig
hid	skid	wig	slid

Concentration

frog	pot	dog	dot
shop	fog	cot	pop
knot	hop	hog	log

Concentration

Word Families: ug, um, ump

gum	grump	plum	drum
mug	slug	glum	bug
lump	rug	jump	yum

Concentration

clock	cash	bank	tank
truck	bunk	shock	sank
block	stuck	trunk	dash

Concentration

Word Families: ake, ale, ame, ate

snake	gate	game	sale
whale	flake	skate	plate
Kate	crate	Jake	bake

Concentration

Word Families: ice, ide, ine, oke, ore

broke	mice	rice	wide
vine	twine	slide	ice
shine	tine	spice	shore

Concentration

pail	train	star	claw
car	jar	Spain	paw
eat	treat	snail	nail

Concentration

Word Families: ing, ay, est, y, ight

wing	swing	light	jay
fry	night	spring	king
fly	dry	knight	nest

Concentration

brick	flip	chin	chick
hip	grin	tack	kink
knit	snack	stick	pack

Word Wheels

Enlarge and photocopy the word wheels and cut apart. Then cut along dots of the window on each wing and fold back. To assemble the word wheels, place the picture on top of the word wheel. Put a paper fastener through the middle of each piece. Invite students to practice all the word families in this book using the variations below.

Variations

◆ Write the beginning sound on the picture page of the word wheel and have the students write the word family ending.

◆ Write the word family ending and have the students write the beginning sound.

◆ Write both the beginning sound and the word family ending and have the students read the words.

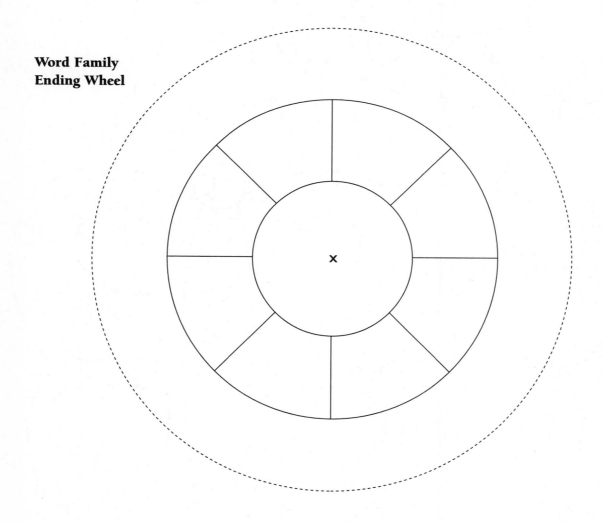

**Word Family
Ending Wheel**

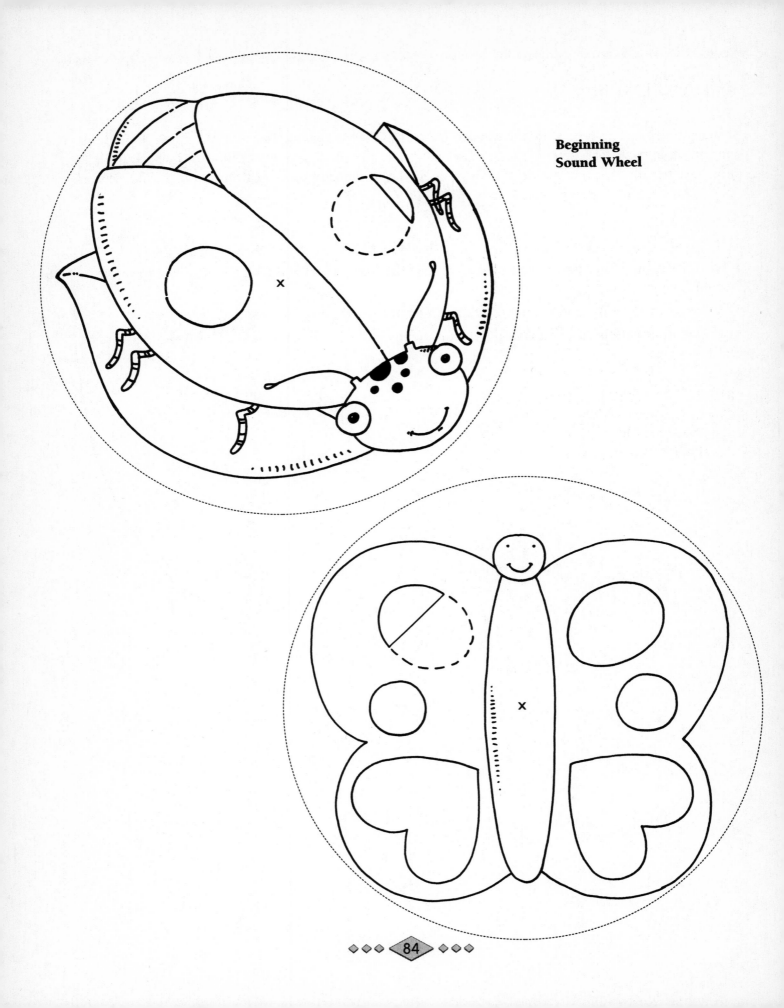

**Beginning
Sound Wheel**

Slide-Throughs

1. Write the beginning and ending sounds on the strips; photocopy.

2. Cut out the strips and cut two slits on the apple.

3. Insert the strips and read the words.

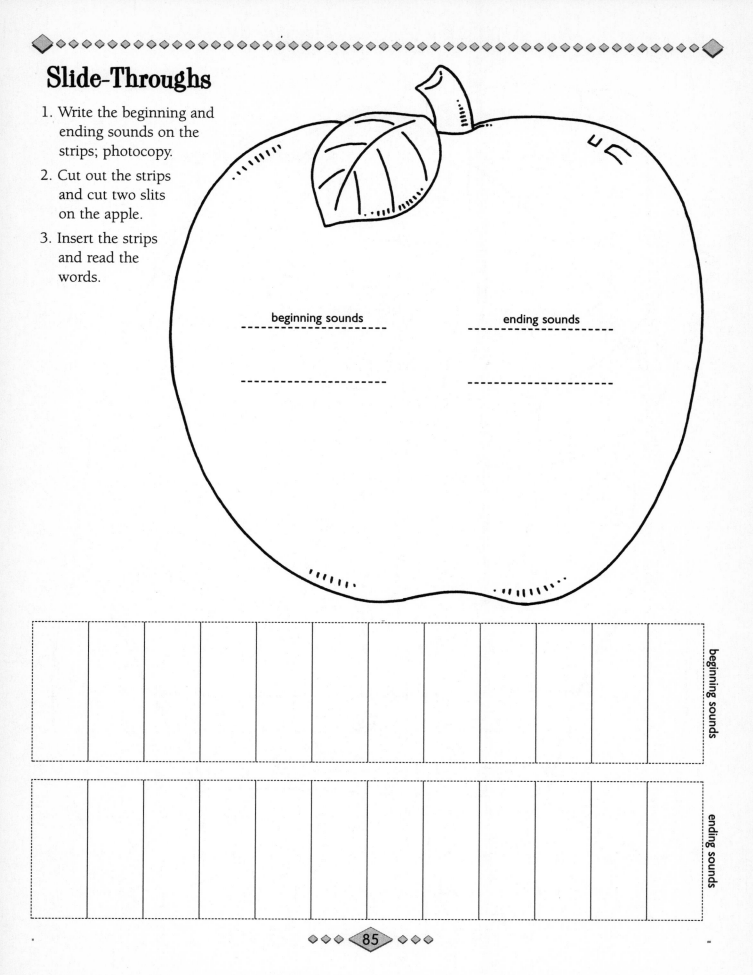

beginning sounds

ending sounds

beginning sounds

ending sounds

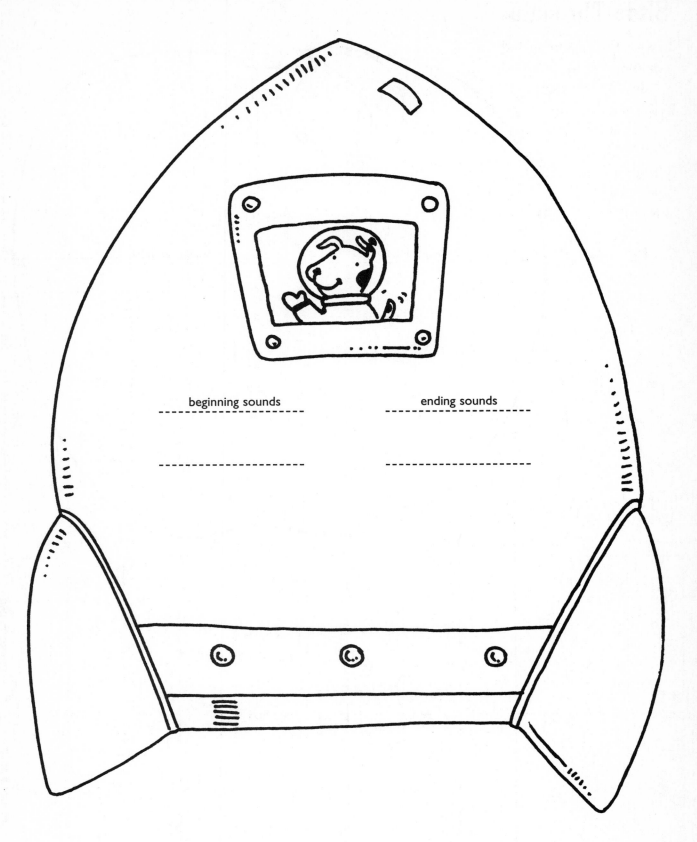

beginning sounds   ending sounds

- - - - - - - - - - - - - - - - - -   - - - - - - - - - - - - - - - - - -

- - - - - - - - - - - - - - - - - -   - - - - - - - - - - - - - - - - - -

Word Family Flip Book

Write the beginning sounds on the left side of each strip and the word family endings on the right side of each strip. (The same word family ending can be used on each strip or several different word families can be used for each flip book.) Photocopy the page and cut out the strips. Staple the beginning sounds onto the right side of a 4" x 6" index card, and the word family endings onto the left side of the index card. The flip book is ready to be read!

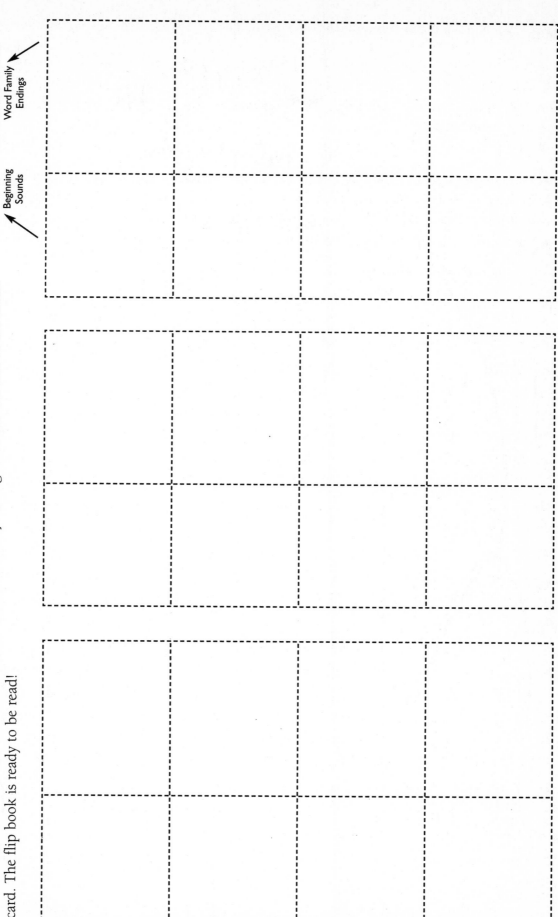

Toss-a-Word

Photocopy (and enlarge, if desired) the game board below. Write a beginning sound or word family ending in each box.

To Play the Game

◆ A student tosses two beans (or cubes, bean bags, pennies, etc.). If the letters in each square that the beans land on make a word, the student earns a point. The next student takes a turn, tossing the two beans onto the board and checking to see if a word is made.

◆ The winner is the one who makes the most words in ten throws or the first person to make ten words.

Puzzle Pieces

Photocopy the selected shapes onto construction paper. Cut out the shapes. On the left side of the shape, write the beginning sound; and on the right side of the shape, write the word family ending. Cut each shape apart. Have the students match the beginning sound shapes to the word family ending to make a word.

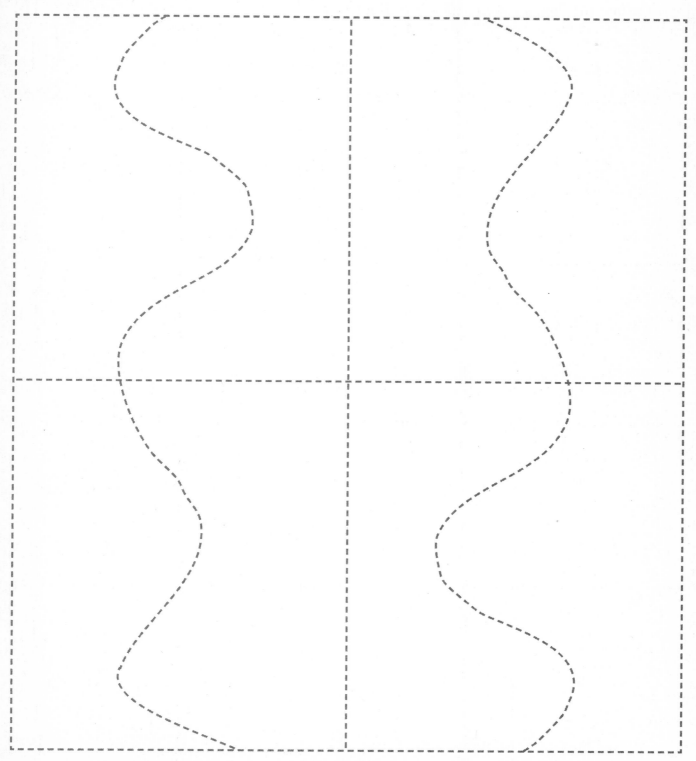

Spin the Wheels!

1. On one wheel, write the beginning sounds.
   On the other wheel, write the ending sounds.

2. Use a paper clip as a spinner (see illustration) and spin both of the spinners. Write the letters on the appropriate line.

3. Circle the letters if they make a real word. Then spin again!

Beginning Sound + Word Family Ending = Word

1. _____ + _____ = _____

2. _____ + _____ = _____

3. _____ + _____ = _____

4. _____ + _____ = _____

5. _____ + _____ = _____

6. _____ + _____ = _____

7. _____ + _____ = _____

8. _____ + _____ = _____

9. _____ + _____ = _____

10. _____ + _____ = _____

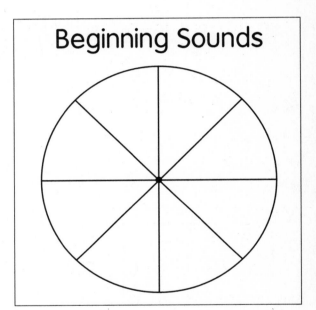

Beginning Sounds

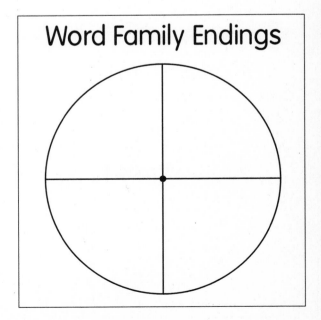

Word Family Endings

Bingo Cards

Cut out the Bingo cards. Practice identifying word family endings and words with this fun variation of the favorite childhood game, Bingo.

Word Family Bingo

	★ Free Space ★	

Word Family Bingo

	★ Free Space ★	

Word Family Bingo

	★ Free Space ★	

Word Family Bingo

	★ Free Space ★	

Blank Flashcards

Cut out the Blank Flashcards. Use them to match beginning sounds with word family endings. You can make lots of words with just one ending!

Name _____

Sort the Words

Your teacher will give you words from two Word Family Activity Sheets.

1. Cut the words apart and mix them up.

2. Sort the words by family. Put all the words in one family in one shape. Put the words of the other family in the other shape.

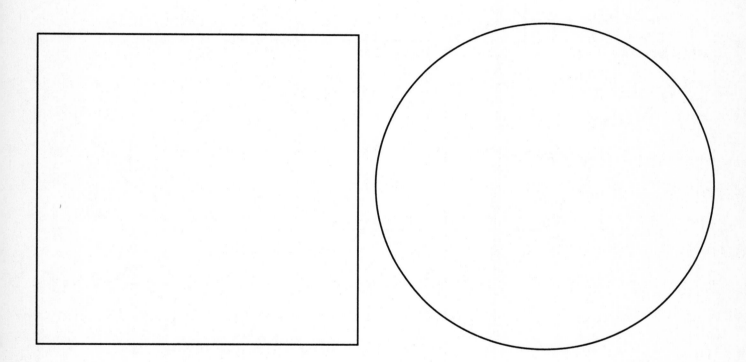

Write sentences. Use one word from each group in each sentence.

1. _____

2. _____

3. _____

4. _____

Word Family Dice

Make two copies of this page. Write beginning sounds on one die. On the other die, write the word family (or families) on each side of the die.

Assembly Instructions:
1. Cut along all outside lines (including in and around large tabs).
2. Fold along all lines.
3. Glue tab A to inside edge of side D.
4. Fold in side flaps.

Directions for Play

Students roll the Word Family Dice and try to form words. Students get one point for each word made. The first one to make six points wins.

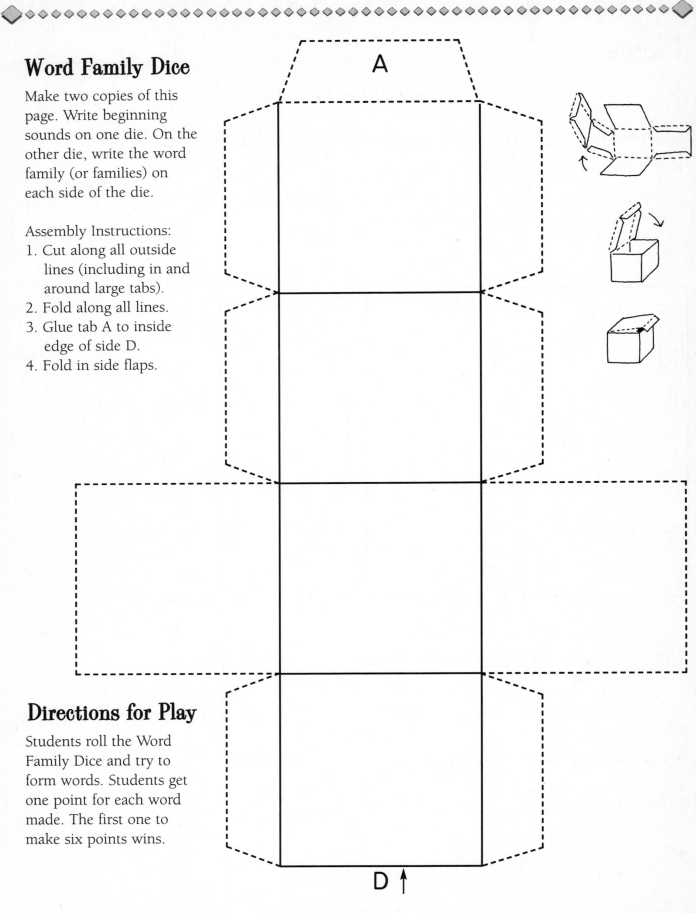

A

D ↑